Tenting by the Cross

The History and Development of the Methodist and Holiness Camp Meeting

By Robert A. Danielson

First Fruits Press
Wilmore, Kentucky
©2019

ISBN: 9781621718659 (print), 9781621718703 (digital), 9781621718710 (kindle)

Tenting by the cross: the history and development of the Methodist and Holiness Camp Meeting.
By Robert A. Danielson.
First Fruits Press, ©2019
Digital version at http://place.asburyseminary.edu/firstfruitsbooks/16

Danielson, Robert A. (Robert Alden), 1969-
    Tenting by the cross : the history and development of the Methodist and holiness camp meeting / by Robert A. Danielson. Wilmore, KY : First Fruits Press, ©2019.

    70 pages : cm
    ISBN: 9781621718659 (pbk.)
    OCLC: 1083260689

    1. Camp-meetings--United States--History. 2. Methodist Church--United States--History. 3. Holiness movement--United States--History.
    4. Methodist preaching--United States--History.

BV3798.D36 2019   269/.24

Cover design by Jon Ramsay

asburyseminary.edu
800.2ASBURY
204 North Lexington Avenue
Wilmore, Kentucky 40390

First Fruits
THE ACADEMIC OPEN PRESS OF ASBURY SEMINARY

First Fruits Press

The Academic Open Press of Asbury Theological Seminary

204 N. Lexington Ave., Wilmore, KY 40390

859-858-2236

first.fruits@asburyseminary.edu

asbury.to/firstfruits

Table of Contents

Chapter 1:

Foundations of Camp Meetings

Beside the Cross I'm tenting,
And I feel a presence there
That touches me with rapture
And heals all my pain and care;
The crimson stream flows over me,
It covers all my sin;
My soul is filled with glory
That my soul and Christ are kin.

Tenting by the Cross (1922)

- Rev. Campbell Coyle (1861-1941)

The camp meeting has been a powerful symbol of frontier religion in the history of the United States of America. Millions of people have attended these gatherings over the years, many finding their Christian faith and salvation in the shady groves, listening to energizing sermons from hastily constructed platforms, crude covered podiums, or simple structures meant to keep the rain out, but still retain the feel of the outside. Traditional hymns, such as "Shall We Gather at the River" and "In the Sweet By-and-By," joined "The Old Rugged Cross" and "I Surrender All" to create a unique evangelistic event. While camp meetings became a trademark of the Methodist and Holiness traditions, their origins go back to the early field preaching of Wesley and Whitefield.

In his journal for Saturday, March 31, 1739, John Wesley notes his first encounter with field preaching,

> In the evening I reached Bristol and met Mr. Whitefield there. I could scarcely reconcile myself at first to this strange way of preaching in the fields, of which he set me an example on Sunday; I had been all my life (till very lately) so tenacious of every point relating to decency and order that I should have thought the saving of souls almost a sin if it had not been done in a church.

Wesley goes on to try field preaching on April 1, 1739, and again on April 2, where he notes, "At four in the afternoon I submitted to be more vile and proclaimed in the highways the glad tidings of salvation, speaking from a little eminence in a ground adjoining to the city to about three thousand people." He also notes preaching to 1,000 in Bristol on April 8th and 1,500 in Kingswood on that same day.

Engraving of John Wesley
Image in the Public domain

Wesley rapidly adapted to this method of field preaching, seeking out areas where it could be most effective, and often preaching from some elevated surface such as a temporary stand, a tree stump, or even a tombstone. Such an approach drew unchurched people, and often loud opposition, but field preaching was exceptionally useful for evangelism. While Wesley considered using this method in place of creating societies, he gave this up because, while it aided evangelistic efforts, it was not useful for further discipleship and spiritual growth. While Wesley preferred to speak indoors, he saw the great advantages of the field preaching approach and encouraged Methodists to adopt this way of evangelizing.[1]

As mentioned by Wesley, it was George Whitefield who really inspired the Methodist fascination with field preaching. With his theatrical flair in preaching, Whitefield found many church doors closed against him in

---

1   Cf. "John Wesley's Principles and Practice of Preaching," by Richard P. Heitzenrater. *Methodist History* (January 1999) 37(2): 89-106.

England, so he took his preaching outside and also developed the style of not reading his sermons, but rather speaking extemporaneously. In 1739, the same year Whitefield introduced Wesley to the method, he also went to the American colonies to speak. Since church buildings could not contain all the people who came to hear him speak, he again moved his preaching outside to large, eager crowds. Whitefield's powerful field preaching would be an instrumental part of the Second Great Awakening.[2] This revival in the American colonies would be the context in which the Methodist camp meeting would begin and flourish.

Engraving of George Whitfield
Image in the Public domain

In part, due to the response to Whitefield's field preaching, as well as the growing number of Methodists who had migrated to the colonies and were establishing societies, the Wesleys sent itinerant preachers to help grow the Christian faith in the American frontier. Circuit riders, like

2   Cf. the special issue of *Christian History* (1993) issue no. 38, "George Whitefield: 17th Century Preacher and Revivalist."

Francis Asbury, road horses between various meeting spots in order to hold quarterly meetings and give the sacraments to Methodists who lived in remote locations. Often these meetings would draw people from various surrounding areas and even from other denominations, and the crowds would overwhelm the small chapels that may have existed in a few of the locations.

Jesse Lee, an early Methodist circuit rider and historian, recalled a 1776 quarterly meeting this way,

> On Tuesday and Wednesday, the 30th and 31st day of July, quarterly meeting was held at Mabur's dwelling house in Brunswick (now Greenville) county. No meeting house in Virginia could have held the people. We had a large arbour in the yard, which would shade from the sun, two or three thousand people. The first day was a blessed season; but the second day was a day never to be forgotten. We held the love feast under the arbour in the open air; the members of society took their seats, and other people stood all around them by hundreds. The place was truly awful, by reason of the presence of the Lord. Many of the members spake; and while some declared how the Lord had justified them freely, others declared how, and when the blood of Jesus had cleansed them all from sin. So clear, so full, and so strong was their testimony, that while some were speaking their experience, hundreds were in tears, and others vehemently crying to God, for pardon or holiness.[3]

Methodist historian, Russell Richey has even reinterpreted early American Methodist history in the light of the themes of "wilderness," "shady grove," and "garden," due to the importance that early Methodist writers seem to place on the emotional and spiritual significance of worship outside of buildings and in natural settings.[4]

The emotional and spiritual power of the natural setting combined with the needs and concerns of early settlers (particularly along the American frontier). This was formalized in the settings of Methodist quarterly meetings, as well as the periodic gatherings of other denominational

---

3   *Methodism in the American Forest* by Russell E. Richey, 2015. New York, NY: Oxford University Press, p. 20.

4   Ibid., p. 94.

ministers in similar frontier settings, and provided the perfect context for the rapid development and spiritual importance of the camp meeting tradition. In many ways, it was a predictable move from the spiritual feeling of the Second Great Awakening as a revival movement, combining with organized religious gatherings outside in natural settings, to the development of the camp meeting as an effective tool for evangelism in the 19th century.

While the gathering of religious people in natural settings was not an uncommon event, these gatherings quickly began to increase in significance. This was not necessarily due to their religious nature. In fact, these large gatherings attracted many people for a variety of reasons. There was an entertainment factor as people gathered to watch the religious eccentricities that were becoming better known in the revival of the Second Great Awakening. There were also people who came for social reasons to trade, exchange the latest news, and also visit with people.

It is difficult to assess if there was a "first" camp meeting. There are at least six permanent camp meeting sites that existed before the Kentucky revival that is usually credited as the beginning of the camp meeting movement. All of these are Methodist in origin and include two in North Carolina (Rock Springs Camp Meeting- founded in 1794, and the Great Union Camp Meeting at Shepherd's Cross Roads in 1796), three in South Carolina (Cypress Camp Meeting- founded in 1794, Cattle Creek Camp Meeting- founded about 1795, and Indian Field Camp Meeting- founded about 1795), and one in Georgia (Effingham County Camp Meeting- founded in 1790). Evidence exists that John McGee, a Methodist minister, was involved in the Rock Springs Camp Meeting, which at the time was known as the Grassy Branch Camp Meeting. It is argued that McGee would take the North Carolina experience with him to Tennessee and this would be the groundwork for the Kentucky revival from which modern camp meetings emerged.[5] Despite various viewpoints, our current view of the camp meeting and its rapid rise in American culture began from the Revival of 1800 and the subsequent Cane Ridge Revival in Kentucky.

---

5   Kenneth O. Brown, *Holy Ground: A Study of the American Camp Meeting*. New York, NY: Garland Publishing, Inc., 1992, pp. 5-22. Brown asserts that John McGee and the Methodists should be credited with the founding of camp meetings and not the Presbyterians of Tennessee and Kentucky.

Chapter 2:
The Cane Ridge Revival

There's a shout in the camp: "Keep the fires brightly burning
All the night long,"
That the lost may return to the fold of the shepherd
From paths of wrong.
There's a shout in the camp, "Hallelujah! Glory to God!"
There's an echo in heav'n, "Hallelujah! Glory to God!"

There's a Shout in the Camp (1905)

- Charles Austin Miles (1868-1946)

In one region of rural Kentucky, in present day Bourbon County near Paris, Kentucky, a log cabin Presbyterian meetinghouse had been constructed by a group of settlers in 1791 in Cane Ridge, Kentucky. It still stands today as the largest single-room log structure in the United States. Built of rough-hewn logs of blue ash, it was built with a large balcony for African-American slaves, who accessed the church by a ladder through an upper window.

Photo of the Original Cane Ridge Meeting House
Image from Library of Congress, Prints & Photographs Division, KY, 9-CANRI, 1-2
Image in the Public Domain

In 1796, a new Presbyterian minister was appointed to the pulpit of the Cane Ridge Meeting-House, as well as a second church in Concord, Kentucky. The young Barton Warren Stone came from North Carolina in 1796 and was opposed to slavery, even freeing slaves he and his family inherited from others. He was also deeply religious and was attracted to reports of a revival coming out of Tennessee into Logan County, Kentucky in the spring of 1801.

Rev. James McGready of the Gaspar River, Red River, and Muddy River Presbyterian congregations apparently started the revival of 1800 in Logan County, Kentucky. He is credited with both the early form of camp meeting that led to the Cane Ridge Revival and also was one of the founders of the Cumberland Presbyterian Church. William McGee was another Presbyterian minister presiding at the Red River Meeting House revival from June 13-17, 1800, and later the Gaspar River Meeting House, along with his brother, John, the Methodist minister previously mentioned at the North Carolina Grassy Branch Camp Meeting. William McGee would also join the Cumberland Presbyterian Church along with McGready. Two other Presbyterian ministers, John Rankin and Rev. William Hodge also took part in the revival of 1800 in Logan County.[6] Stone was impressed by this revival, and so he organized a similar revival to be held at Cane Ridge from August 7-12, 1801. Stone arranged to hold this revival with the cooperation of Methodist and Baptist pastors in the area. The revival exceeded any expectations! An earlier revival in Concord had numbered between 7,000 and 8,000 people, but the Cane Ridge Revival has been estimated to have drawn between 20,000 and 30,000 people.[7]

The tents were arranged like city blocks extending over a mile in every direction around the meetinghouse and through the canebrakes that gave this area its name. There were five to seven different preaching points around the encampment for the preachers of different backgrounds to speak to the crowds. One writer records the event this way,

> The spectacle presented at night was one of the wildest grandeur. The glare of the blazing camp-fires falling on a dense multitude of heads, simultaneously bowed in adoration, and reflected back from the long range of tents upon every side, hundreds of lamps and candles suspended among the trees, together with numerous torches flashing to and fro, throwing an uncertain light upon the tremulous foliage and giving an appearance of dim and indefinite extent to the depth of the forest; the solemn chanting of hymns, swelling and falling on the night winds; the impassioned exhortations, the earnest prayers, the sobs, the shrieks or shouts bursting from persons under agitation of mind; the sudden spasms which seized upon and unexpectedly

---

6   Information from the Red River Meeting House web site: http://www.rrmh.org/ history.

7   Cf. *The Cane Ridge Meeting-house* by James R. Rogers, 1910.Cincinnati, OH: The Standard Publishing Company, pp. 52-62.

dashed them to the ground- all conspired to invest the scene with terrific interest, and arouse their feelings to the highest state of excitement.[8]

Stone would note his own version of the Cane Ridge Revival this way,

> The roads were literally crowded with wagons, carriages, horsemen, and footmen, moving to the solemn camp. The sight was affecting. It was judged by military men on the ground, that there were between twenty and thirty thousand collected. Four or five preachers were frequently speaking at the same time in different parts of the encampment, without confusion. The Methodist and Baptist preachers aided in the work, and all appeared cordially united in it- of one mind and one soul, and the salvation of sinners seemed to be the great object of all. We all engaged in singing the same songs of praise- all united in prayer- all preached the same things- free salvation urged upon all by faith and repentance. A particular description of this meeting would fill a large volume, and then the half would not be told. The numbers converted will be known only in eternity. Many things transpired there, which were so much like miracles, that if they were not, they had the same effects as miracles on infidels and unbelievers; for many of them were convinced that Jesus was the Christ, and bowed in submission to him. This meeting continued six or seven days and nights, and would have continued longer, but provisions for such a multitude failed in the neighborhood.[9]

Stone goes on to describe some of the "religious exercises" of the time. They went by such names as the "falling exercise," the "jerks," the "dancing exercise," the "barking exercise," and the "laughing and singing exercise." Spontaneous accounts of people falling over in the Spirit into a death-like state, rapid jerking movements of the body and face (to which Barton also attributes the "barking" sounds), unconscious dancing movements,

8   *The Cane Ridge Meeting-house*, by James R. Rogers, 1910. Cincinnati, OH: The Standard Publishing Company, pp. 56.

9   *The Biography of Eld. Barton Warren Stone, Written by Himself, with Additions and Reflections*, by Elder John Rogers, 1847. Cincinnati, OH: J.A. and U.P. James, pp. 37-38

spontaneous laughing or running back and forth, and an odd heavenly singing done not with mouth or nose, but seeming to come from the chest, are just some of the actions that occurred. It was often reports of these behaviors that also brought curiosity seekers to these early revivals for entertainment.[10]

Bust of Barton Stone at the Cane Ridge Site, near Paris, KY
Image taken by staff of B.L. Fisher Library

Methodist pastor, James B. Finley, the son of the first pastor of the Cane Ridge Meeting-house, was one person who attended the Cane Ridge Revival as a young man of twenty who lacked a conversion experience. In an account of his life he wrote,

> In the month of August, 1801, I learned that there was to be a great meeting at Cane Ridge, in my father's old congregation. Feeling a great desire to see the wonderful things which had come to my ears, and having been

---

10 Ibid., pp. 39-42.

solicited by some of my old schoolmates to go over into Kentucky for the purpose of revisiting the scenes of my boyhood, I resolved to go…

We arrived upon the ground, and here a scene presented itself to my mind not only novel and unaccountable, but awful beyond description. A vast crowd, supposed by some to have amounted to twenty-five thousand, was collected together. The noise was like the roar of Niagara. The vast sea of human beings seemed to be agitated as if by a storm. I counted seven ministers, all preaching at one time, some on stumps, others in wagons, and one -- the Rev. William Burke, now of Cincinnati -- was standing on a tree which had, in falling, lodged against another. Some of the people were singing, others praying, some crying for mercy in the most piteous accents, while others were shouting most vociferously. While witnessing these scenes, a peculiarly-strange sensation, such as I had never felt before, came over me. My heart beat tumultuously, my knees trembled, my lip quivered, and I felt as though I must fall to the ground. A strange supernatural power seemed to pervade the entire mass of mind there collected…

After some time I returned to the scene of excitement, the waves of which, if possible, had risen still higher. The same awfulness of feeling came over me. I stepped up on to a log, where I could have a better view of the surging sea of humanity. The scene that then presented itself to my mind was indescribable. At one time I saw at least five hundred swept down in a moment, as if a battery of a thousand guns had been opened upon them, and then immediately followed shrieks and shouts that rent the very heavens…[11]

In 1804, Stone would lead the Cane Ridge congregation and others out of the Presbyterian Church and with Alexander Campbell, the Stone-Campbell movement would eventually become the Christian Church (Disciples of Christ) in 1832. This movement struggled against

---

11 *Pioneer Life in the West: The Autobiography of James Bradley Finley*, edited by W. P. Strickland, 1853. Cincinnati, OH: Cranston and Curts. Digital version accessed at: http://wesley.nnu.edu/wesleyctr/books/0601-0700/HDM0683.pdf (pages 79-80 of the digital version).

denominationalism, which created disunity, especially among Christian believers at the communion table. Some of this feeling can be traced back to Stone's experience at Cane Ridge.

Interior of the Cane Ridge Meeting House, near Paris, KY
Image taken by staff of B.L. Fisher Library

While this movement was distinctly separate from the Methodist Movement and its subsequent camp meeting tradition, it was an essential part of the revivalism that led to a growing interest in camp meetings among Methodists and those in other traditions. Its interdenominational character, which included the presence of Methodist as well as Baptist ministers, may also help account for the growth of camp meetings among the early Methodists. News of this large revival in rural Kentucky spread rapidly, and what began as a revival with tents used out of necessity would grow into the revivalist camp meeting of the later 19th century.

Chapter 3:

The Growth of Early Methodist Camp Meetings

Shall we gather at the river, where bright angel feet have trod;
With its crystal tide forever, flowing by the throne of God?
Yes, we'll gather at the river, the beautiful, beautiful river.
Gather with the saints at the river that flows by the throne of God!

Shall We Gather at the River (1864)

- Rev. Robert Lowry (1826-1899)

Methodists were not only involved in both the Logan County Revival of 1800 (with Methodist John McGee as part of the group of preachers) and the 1801 Cane Ridge Revival, but in between these events, in October of 1800, Methodist Bishop Francis Asbury was also on the scene in Tennessee. From his journal for Saturday, October 18th, Asbury records meeting with the Brothers McGee along with other local pastors in Tennessee and notes, "we had a small shout in the camp of Israel." On Monday, October 20, 1800, Asbury records meeting Hodge, Rankin, McGee and other Presbyterian leaders at Drake's Creek Meeting-house. These were three of McGready's helpers in the 1800 revival. It is here that Asbury gets his first taste of a camp meeting. On the 21st, Asbury writes,

> Yesterday, and especially during the night, were witnessed scenes of deep interest. In the intervals between preaching, the people refreshed themselves and horses, and returned upon the ground. The stand was in the open air, embosomed in the wood of lofty beech trees. The ministers of God, Methodists and Presbyterians, united their labors, and mingled with the childlike simplicity of primitive times. Fires blazing here and there dispelled the darkness, and the shouts of the redeemed captives, and the cries of precious souls struggling into life, broke the silence of midnight. The weather was delightful; as if heaven smiled, whilst mercy flowed in abundant streams of salvation to perishing sinners. We suppose there were at least thirty souls converted at this meeting. I rejoice that God is visiting the sons of the Puritans, who are candid enough to acknowledge their obligations to the Methodists.

Asbury continues in the next few days to refer again to both William and John McGee during his time in Tennessee.[12] It can only be assumed that during this time, Asbury both heard and experienced people's responses to the Logan County revival of 1800, which happened just four months previously.

---

12 From *The Journal of the Rev. Francis Asbury, Bishop of the Methodist Episcopal Church, From August 7, 1771, to December 7, 1815,* by Francis Asbury. New York, NY: N. Bangs and T. Mason, 1821, Vol. 2, pp. 395-398.

Engraving of Francis Asbury
Image in the Public Domain

From the 1801 Cane Ridge Revival, the idea of evangelistic camp meetings began to take shape. Historian Darius Salter notes that the cooperation between Methodists and Presbyterians had broken down by 1806, and so the Methodists adopted their own form of the permanent camp meeting.[13] Francis Asbury is even recorded in a letter to Jacob Gruber in 1811 stating, "Doubtless, if the state and provinces hold twelve million, we congregate annually 3 if not 4 million in campmeetings! The battle ax and weapon of war, it will break down walls of wickedness, part of hell, superstitious, false doctrine…" Scott Cole notes that by 1811 there were more that 500 camp meetings being held annually, and by 1820 the number reached 1,600- just 19 years after the Cane Ridge Revival![14]

---

13 Darius Salter, *America's Bishop: The Life of Francis Asbury.* Nappanee, IN: Evangel Publishing House, 2003, pp246-248.

14 Scott W. Cole, *Traumatized Performance: Antebellum Methodist Camp Meetings and the Re-Making of the American Frontier.* Ph.D. dissertation at the University of Washington.

Camp Meeting (circa. 1832) Oil on Pine Panels, by Alexander Rider

Image used Courtesy of Special Collections, Buswell Library, Wheaton College

These early camp meetings often relied on crudely constructed preaching platforms and rough benches. People brought tents and supplies in order to attend and care for their own needs. Spiritually, these were emotional events. A record of the life of John Allen (also known as "Camp Meeting John" because of his involvements with camp meetings throughout his life) notes the account the author heard from John Allen about his own initial camp meeting experience in 1825 in Industry, Maine:

> The writer of this sketch once heard him (John Allen) say that as he was going to the camp meeting, he earnestly prayed that if he was mistaken in his religious belief he might be convinced of his error at the meeting.
>
> The meeting was in a forest in the easterly part of Industry, on the land of Captain Thompson, exceedingly primitive in all its appointments. The preachers' stand was rudely constructed of poles and unplanned boards at very small expense. The seats were rough planks resting upon logs. There were some fifteen or sixteen society tents of cotton cloth stretched upon frames, which served for dining-rooms at meal times, lodging at night, and for prayer meeting in the intermediate periods.
>
> The preaching was earnest, the prayers ardent, and the singing hearty. The grove resounded with songs of praise and shouts of joy. Mr. Allen was much interested in the services, and soon became deeply convicted of his sins and of his appalling danger. Upon invitation of Father Newell, he went forward, knelt at the altar and earnestly sought for pardon. He continued for some time seeking, his distress became overwhelming. He arose and earnestly entreated all who had access to the throne of grace to pray for him, till at length his mind became calm. He ventured to say, "there is peace," when immediately he was filled with rapture, and rushed up the aisle like the lame man in scripture, "leaping and praising God."
>
> This was no transient excitement. The change was thorough and abiding. The whole course of his life was reversed. His joy was "unspeakable." He immediately commenced an earnest Christian life, and declared to all whom he met what great things the Lord had done for him; and to the

Photograph of Early Primitive Camp Meeting, Location Unknown (circa. 1890)
Image from the Archives and Special Collections of B.L. Fisher Library, Asbury Theological Seminary

close of his life he always loved to rehearse the wonderful deliverance he received at this memorable camp meeting. Ever after, the camp meeting seemed to him the next place to heaven.[15]

In an account published by Frances Milton Trollope in 1832, the English woman visiting the United States set out to visit and describe an early camp meeting in Indiana in detail. She did not find it a very agreeable visit, but did describe the event through her British eyes:

> We reached the ground about an hour before midnight, and the approach to it was highly picturesque. The spot chosen was the verge of an unbroken forest, where a space of about twenty acres appeared to have been partially cleared for the purpose. Tents of different sizes were pitched very near together in a circle round the cleared space; behind them were ranged an exterior circle of carriages of every description, and at the back of each were fastened the horses which had drawn them thither. Through this triple circle of defense we distinguished numerous fires burning brightly within it; and still more numerous lights flickering from the trees that were left in the enclosure. The moon was in meridian splendor above our heads.

> We left the carriage to the care of a servant, who was to prepare a bed in it for Mrs. B. and me, and entered the inner circle. The first glance reminded me of Vauxhall, from the effect of the lights among the trees, and the moving crowd below them; but the second showed a scene totally unlike any thing I had ever witnessed. Four high frames, constructed in the forms of altars, were placed at the four corners of the enclosure; on these were supported layers of earth and sod, on which burned immense fires of blazing pine-wood. On one side a rude platform was erected to accommodate the preachers, fifteen of whom attended this meeting, and with very short intervals for necessary refreshment and private devotion, preached in rotation, day and night, from Tuesday to Saturday.

---

15   Rev. Stephen Allen, *The Life of Rev. John Allen, Better Known as "Camp Meeting John."* Boston. MA: B.B. Russell, 1888, pp. 21-23.

When we arrived, the preachers were silent; but we heard issuing from nearly every tent mingled sounds of praying, preaching, singing, and lamentation. The curtains in front of each tent were dropped, and the faint light that gleamed through the white drapery, backed as it was by the dark forest, had a beautiful and mysterious effect, that set the imagination at work; and had the sounds which vibrated around us been less discordant, harsh, and unnatural, I should have enjoyed it; but listening at the corner of a tent which poured forth more than its proportion of clamour, in a few moments chased every feeling derived from imagination, and furnished realities that could neither be mistaken or forgotten.

Great numbers of persons were walking about the ground, who appeared like ourselves to be present only as spectators; some of these very unceremoniously contrived to raise the drapery of this tent at one corner, so as to afford us a perfect view of the interior.

The floor was covered with straw, which round the sides was heaped in masses, that might serve as seats, but which at the moment were used to support the heads and the arms of the close-packed circle of men and women who kneeled on the floor…

We made the circuit of the tents, pausing where attention was particularly excited by sounds more vehement than ordinary. We contrived to look into many; all were strewed with straw, and the distorted figures that we saw kneeling, sitting, and lying among it, joined to the woeful and convulsive cries, gave to each the air of a cell in Bedlam.

One tent was occupied exclusively by Negroes. They were all full-dressed, and looked exactly as if they were preforming a scene on the stage. One woman wore a dress of pink gauze trimmed with silver lace; another was dressed in pale yellow silk; one or two had splendid turbans; and all wore a profusion of ornaments. The men were in snow white pantaloons, with gay coloured linen jackets. One of these, a youth of coal-black comeliness, was preaching with the most violent gesticulations, frequently springing high from the ground, and clapping his hands over his head...

At midnight, a horn sounded through the camp, which we were told, was to call the people from private to public worship; and we presently saw them flocking from all sides to the front of the preachers' stand... There were about two thousand persons assembled...

"The pen" was the space immediately below the preachers' stand; we were therefore placed on the edge of it, and were enabled to see and hear all that took place in the very centre of this extraordinary exhibition.

The crowd fell back at the mention of the pen, and for some minutes there was a vacant space before us. The preachers came down from their stand, and placed themselves in the midst of it, beginning to sing a hymn, calling upon the penitents to come forth. As they sung they kept turning themselves round to every part of the crowd, and, by degrees, the voices of the whole multitude joined in chorus. This was the only moment at which I perceived any thing like the solemn and beautiful effect which I had heard ascribed to this woodland worship. It is certain that the combined voices of such a multitude, heard at dead of night, from the depths of their eternal forests, the many fair young faces turned upward, and looking paler and lovelier as they met the moonbeams, the dark figures of the officials in the middle of the circle, the lurid glare thrown by the altar fires on the woods beyond, did altogether produce a fine and solemn effect, that I shall not easily forget; but ere I had well enjoyed it, the scene changed, and sublimity gave place to horror and disgust.

The exhortation nearly resembled that which I had heard at "the revival," but the result was very different; for, instead of a few hysterical women who had distinguished themselves on that occasion, above a hundred persons, nearly all females, came forward, uttering howling and groans so terrible that I shall never cease to shudder when I recall them. They appeared to drag each other forward, and on the word being given, "let us pray," they all fell on their knees; but this posture was soon changed for others that permitted greater scope for the convulsive movements of their limbs; and they were soon all lying on the ground in an indescribable confusion of heads and legs. They threw about their limbs with such incessant and violent motion, that I was every instant expecting some serious accident to occur.

But how am I to describe the sounds that proceeded from this strange mass of human beings? I know no words which can convey an idea of it. Hysterical sobbings, convulsive groans, shrieks and screams the most appalling burst forth on all sides. I felt sick with horror. As if their hoarse and overstrained voices failed to make noise enough, they soon began to clap their hands violently.[16]

These early camp meeting events were scenes of great spiritual revival, held in primitive conditions. But their spiritual power and influence kept people returning to the same places year after year. Thus stable permanent places for camp meetings were established and gradually tents began to be replaced by buildings for worship or dining, and then small permanent dwellings began to replace the tents of individual families. These spiritual events began to be transformed into popular vacation or holiday destinations, and the spiritual meaning began to take secondary importance.

---

16 Frances Milton Trollope, *Domestic Manners of the Americans*. London: Printed for Whittaker, Treacher, and Co., 1832, pp. 139-144.

Chapter 4:

The Domestication of Methodist Camp Meetings

Hover o'er me, Holy Spirit, Bathe my trembling heart and brow;
Fill me with Thy hallowed presence, Come, O come and fill me
now.
Fill me now, fill me now, Jesus, come and fill me now;
Fill me with Thy hallowed presence, Come, O come, and fill me
now.

Fill Me Now (1879)

- Elwood Haines Stokes (1815-1897)
President of the Ocean Grove Camp Meeting Association

To really understand the "domestication" of the camp meeting, it might be helpful to trace the history of just one of these camp meeting locations. One of the most prominent camp meeting spots in New England was Wesleyan Grove on Martha's Vineyard, Massachusetts.

The earliest camp meeting was held in what became Wesleyan Grove in 1835. An early history of the camp meeting notes,

> The ground had been leased, and a portion of it cleared of underbrush. A rough shed was erected for the preachers' stand, the interior of which was their lodging-room, rye straw being furnished for their bedding. Fortunate was he of the "cloth" who could get an extra bundle for his pillow. The seats for the audience were of plain, rough boards, without backs. The entire area cleared was small, and but nine tents graced the circle. Some of these were quite rudely constructed. A few hundred people attended; probably not over a thousand heard preaching at any one time.[17]

"Camp Meeting" John Allen came down from Maine to preach at the camp meeting in 1839. By 1857 there were over 250 tents and 60 different ministers in attendance.

By 1859, Wesleyan Grove began some significant changes. Wooden buildings were constructed to store tents, for business meetings, and house visiting speakers, roads were established (and given names) and tents were set out like a small village. A source for fresh water was established as well as a small police force. A steamer brought visitors to the island for the camp meeting daily. An outside report praised their order and effectiveness and added,

> When I first visited the encampment on Sunday last, there were probably, twenty thousand persons assembled within a circuit of three miles; and although the day was the blessed Sabbath, the scene, for a few hours, reminded me of the Fourth of July, minus fireworks and boisterousness. Everybody appeared happy, joyful, smiling; thousands of young and beautiful females, elegantly dressed,

---

17 Rev. H. Vincent, *History of the Camp-Meeting and Grounds at Wesleyan Grove, Martha's Vineyard, For Eleven Years Ending with the Meeting of 1869*. Boston, MA: Lee and Shepard, 1870, pp. 15-16.

Photograph of Willimantic Camp Meeting, Connecticut (circa. 1915) - An Example of a "Domesticated Camp Meeting"

Image from the Archives and Special Collections of B.L. Fisher Library, Asbury Theological Seminary

promenaded along green paths with young men, whilst an immense crowd listened attentively to eloquent and deeply impressive addresses from clergymen, whose only object appeared to be to save souls.

Many thousand persons visited the camp meeting merely to enjoy a day's pleasure, and seemed to take not the slightest interest in the religious services; but not one individual interfered in any manner to interrupt or disturb the true worshippers beneath the bright-silver-and-blue canopy of heaven. There was a sacred circle of Christians within the great outside crowd, from whence went up to the great God fervent prayers from the heart, and great and ever-living biblical truths.[18]

In 1860, a constitution was established to organize the Martha's Vineyard Camp Meeting Association and it was also noted that many of the tents that year used board sides and cloth tops. The committee overseeing the camp meeting also decided that year to build a new covered preacher's stand, provide for additional lighting, and pay a man to be a year-round caretaker of the campground. An outsider described the new tents,

There are more than five hundred tents, all told, being at least sixty more than were ever built before. Many of the tents are made of wood, the boards being grooved and tongued, well shingled, made perfectly watertight, with a ventilator on the top, finished elegantly, even to knobs on the outside doors.[19]

In 1861 there were new buildings including a refreshment stand and a photographer's building so people could have their pictures taken. While preaching and singing continued, along with religious exercises and a life ordered by the ringing of a bell, there are no real reports about the type of religious excitement or fervor of the early days. By 1862, cottages are being mentioned as well as permanent tent frames and wooden floors, which were left all year round. While "Camp Meeting" John Allen and other speakers seem to keep to solid religious teaching, the presence of military and political leaders also begins to be recognized.

---

18 Ibid., p. 42.
19 Ibid., p. 61.

Stereograph Image of Early Cottages in Wesleyan Grove
Image from the Boston Public Library with Creative Commons Attribution License

In 1864 the campground was divided up into lots and by 1866 cottages had replaced many of the older tents, and these cottages were becoming more elaborate and fashionable. In discussing this year, Vincent notes,

> We, of course, admit that many have tents and cottages here who are not professors of experimental religion, and not a few who are not connected with Methodist congregations at home; but they are usually people of high respectability, of good morals and character. And, coming to a place which they know is selected and held for religious purposes, they conform themselves to its prescribed rules, so that even during the weeks spent here before the time of the camp meeting proper, Christian people who are here are the controlling element in the society of the place, holding frequent evening prayer meetings, and having preaching on the holy Sabbath.[20]

In 1865 the campground was finally officially purchased by the Camp Meeting Association instead of leased. In 1866, just the next year, a group of investors, calling themselves the Oak Bluffs Land and Wharf Company, purchased much of the remaining property around the campground,

20 Ibid., p. 129

including all of the land between the campground and the beach. This company set out to create a new town of Oak Bluffs in part based on the growing fame of Wesleyan Grove.[21] Henry Beetle Hough describes the social setting at the time,

> As cottages succeeded tents, the informality and intimacy were hardly lessened. Most of the cottages were developed by obvious steps from the tent idea. They had wide doors, like church doors, which opened to expose the entire interior of the cottages themselves, thus admitting all possible fresh air, preserving the idea of life in the open, and putting the family life forever on display. One passed under the trees, through winding walks, around circles, and everywhere could not fail to observe what the cottages were doing- whether meals were being served, or daughters were lying in hammocks reading, or mothers sitting with their sewing, or social gatherings exchanging the gossip of the day.[22]

The religious leaders of Wesleyan Grove battled the new owners of Oak Bluffs. In April of 1867 the Oak Bluffs Company agreed to sell and lease its lots in line with the restrictions of the Camp Meeting Association. Nevertheless, the Camp Meeting Association put up a seven-foot high picket fence around its entire 36-acre campground. This was complete with gates that were closed and locked at 10:00 pm and did not reopen until morning. In addition, they purchased an additional 55 acres on the other side of the campground to protect themselves from being completely surrounded by the town of Oak Bluffs in 1869.[23] In the same year a large tent was added to cover the people attending services. One writer records life in the campground in 1868 this way,

> The Martha's Vineyard Camp Ground may truly be called a city in the woods- a religious watering-place on a huge scale, as nearly every State in the Union is represented. The majority of the cottages are inhabited during the months of June, July, and August, and many families remain until October. The following programme will give you an idea of

21 Henry Beetle Hough, *Martha's Vineyard: Summer Resort 1835-1935*. Rutland, VT, The Tuttle Publishing Company, Inc., 1936, p. 61.
22 Ibid., p. 65.
23 Ibid., pp. 67-68.

what we do daily at the Vineyard. The gong sounds precisely at half past six A.M. We have breakfast at seven, morning prayer at eight, in a huge tent seating about one thousand persons; bathe at nine; dine at twelve; go sailing, fishing, blueberrying, or rambling on the beach for shells or odd stones in the afternoon; tea, six P.M.; preaching, or prayer-meeting, or experience meeting every evening. On Sundays we have three sermons from three different preachers, who are stopping on the ground. These meetings are only preliminary to the grand finale, which will commence on Monday the 24th of August and continue until the 2nd day of September.[24]

Stereograph Image Showing Second Preaching Stand and Tent for the Public

Image from the Boston Public Library with Creative Commons Attribution License

Rev. H. Vincent even takes some time in his book promoting Wesleyan Grove to lament the changes over time. He writes,

Is it a reality? Am I really in the old Wesleyan Grove? Or am I in some fairy-land? It must be the same old place; but,

24 Rev. H. Vincent, *History of the Camp-Meeting and Grounds at Wesleyan Grove, Martha's Vineyard, For Eleven Years Ending with the Meeting of 1869*. Boston, MA: Lee and Shepard, 1870, pp. 219-220.

O, how changed! The old oak forest, which I entered, with a few others about thirty-two years ago, for the purpose of selecting a spot for the camp–meeting site, has been cleared of underbrush, and become densely populated over broad acres. Instead of the few hundreds of poor, humble followers of the Master, who came here to worship, dwelling in rough tents, we have now, it is true, a remnant, a sprinkling of those, but mostly those of fashion, and many of large wealth.[25]

Oak Bluffs would become a classic Victorian seaside resort. Hotels, boarding houses, and entertainments of all kinds began to spring up in the building boom of this vacation spot by the ocean. In 1876, the fame of Oak Bluffs was such that it became the site of a presidential visit by President Ulysses S. Grant, along with his wife, the Vice President, the Postmaster General, and the Governor of Massachusetts. The President and his party stayed at the cottage of Bishop Haven on the campground. Brass bands, fireworks, and decorations of all kinds celebrated the president's visit, but the president was also present at the love feast and services held in the tabernacle of the old camp meeting site.[26]

Stereograph Image of Victorian Cottages in Wesleyan Grove
Image from the Boston Public Library with Creative Commons Attribution License

25   Ibid., pp. 178-179.
26   Henry Beetle Hough, *Martha's Vineyard: Summer Resort 1835-1935*. Rutland, VT, The Tuttle Publishing Company, Inc., 1936, pp. 114-116.

In 1879, the tent and preacher's stand was replaced with an open wooden tabernacle, which was added to the National Register of Historic Places in 1979. However, from the time of President Grant's visit on, the role of the Wesleyan Grove Camp Meeting faded as the summer resort of Oak Bluffs boomed. In 1887, the religious leaders briefly tried to prevent the sale of alcoholic beverages, but by 1888, the town was open to the sale of alcohol and the role of the religious people of the camp meeting effectively ended.[27] Oak Bluffs would become known as a tourist destination and the campgrounds became a site to visit with its quaint gingerbread cottages and a feeling of Victorian nostalgia.

Postcard of the Wooden Tabernacle that Replaced the Tent
Image from the Boston Public Library with Creative Commons Attribution License

Wesleyan Grove was not unique in its "domestication." Other campgrounds became places for people to take summer vacations with various social activities and occasionally speakers, who might be religious. Ocean Grove, New Jersey and Old Orchard Beach, Maine are two well-known examples that followed the pattern of "domestication" seen at Wesleyan Grove. Tabernacles became part of Chautauqua-type entertainments, even if Sunday worship services might still be held in the structures themselves. In fact, the entire Chautauqua movement can be seen as a part of this "domestication" of the camp meeting, as it emerged

27 Ibid., pp. 182-185.

in 1872 and 1873 as a "camp meeting that was not a camp meeting" or a "Sunday School camp meeting." It often developed on the sites of former Methodist religious camp meetings. The camp meeting itself might even exist in some of these places, but often as a specially designated week in an entire summer's worth of special events and activities. The spiritual vitality of the camp meeting movement was clearly waning by the 1870s and 1880s.

Chapter 5:

The Christian Holiness Association and the Revival of Camp Meetings

I long ago left Egypt for the promised land,
I trusted in my Savior, and to His guiding hand;
He led me out to vict'ry through the great Red Sea,
I sang a song of triumph, and shouted, "I am free!"
You need not look for me, down in Egypt's land,
For I have pitched my tent far up in Beulah land;
You need not look for me, down in Egypt's land,
For I have pitched my tent far up in Beulah land!

I've Pitched My Tent in Beulah (1908)

- Margaret Jenkins Harris (1865-1919)

As many of the traditional camp meetings were fading in their spiritual vitality, others were rethinking the role of the camp meeting in American spirituality. In 1866 a small group of Methodist leaders connected to the Holiness Movement, including Rev. John A. Wood, William B. Osborn, and Rev. John S. Inskip, met and organized the National Camp Meeting Association for the Promotion of Holiness. They held their first national camp meeting in July of 1867 at Vineland, New Jersey and Rev. John S. Inskip was elected as president. It is estimated that 10,000 people came to hear Methodist Bishop Matthew Simpson. The second national camp meeting in 1868 at Manheim, Pennsylvania drew closer to 25,000 people, with the third national camp meeting held in 1869 at Round Lake, New York solidifying the movement as a major spiritual force in the country.[28]

Photograph of Douglas Holiness Camp Meeting, Massachusetts (July 1890) Rev. John A. Wood is Present on the Bridge along with Bishop William Taylor

Image from the Archives and Special Collections of B.L. Fisher Library, Asbury Theological Seminary

In 1870, the organization purchased a tent and planned three major camp meetings in strategic areas of the country. They also began production of a periodical, *The Advocate of Christian Holiness*, in the same year. After

28 Kenneth O. Brown, *Holy Ground: A Study of the American Camp Meeting.* New York, NY: Garland Publishing, Inc., 1992, p. 33.

Inskip's death in 1884, William McDonald, the editor of *The Advocate for Christian Holiness* was named the president of the organization. In 1894, Charles J. Fowler was named the new president.

This period of time from about 1890 to 1920 was a period of great growth and expansion for the holiness camp meeting. With the organizational effort of what became the Christian Holiness Association and the rise of local holiness organizations, regular meetings were established to promote the teaching of holiness. Evangelists and revivalists travelled extensively, especially during the summer months to speak to large crowds at local camp meetings. Names such as Seth Cook Rees, "Uncle Bud" Robinson, Beverly Carradine, John Haywood Paul, William Bramwell Osborn, Henry Clay Morrison, and George McLaughlin emerge out of this time period, as well as a host of other holiness writers, evangelists, and missionaries.

Martin Wells Knapp at God's Bible College experimented with the idea of visual images and analogies in his teaching and preaching, and other students of his followed in the same pattern, including Arthur Greene, a camp meeting evangelist in New England and along the East Coast. Several of his large camp meeting painted canvases are in the Archives and Special Collections of B.L. Fisher Library at Asbury Theological Seminary.

Image from a Tin Tray of Arthur Greene and the Tabernacle at the Hebron Campground in Massachusetts (circa. 1910)
Item from the Archives and Special Collections of B.L. Fisher Library,
Asbury Theological Seminary

One such illustration seems to be connected to a sermon of some kind, but the original sermon text seems to be lost. The painting shows fourteen birds in relation to a single tree. Some of the birds have human features and seem to represent specific types of people. This illustration or one similar to it may be alluded to in a sermon at the Portsmouth, Rhode Island Camp meeting of 1897. This camp meeting was founded by Seth Rees and was very close to where Greene was born and ministered, so it is likely to have been a major influence in his ministry in New England. In a sermon by Rev. Beverly Carradine on Saturday, August 7, 1897, he speaks on the relevant topic of the day that people from the Holiness Movement were splitting the Methodist Church in a brief aside,

> They say we are splitting the church, but we are not. The truth never splits the true church. God says the kingdom of heaven is like unto a mustard seed. If Colonel Buzzard and Judge Crow and Sister Woodpecker, President of the Ladies Aid Society, are the 'fowls of the air' who are in the branches, no doubt the double-barreled shot-gun of a full salvation minister will disturb *them*, but it will not hurt the tree.[29]

While there are many examples of written and published camp meeting sermons, especially from the holiness tradition, this brief example shows how speakers of the era appealed to the people both through visual and verbal illustrations.

In 1899 the organization changed its name to the National Association for the Promotion of Holiness. Kenneth Brown has noted,

> The association's annual business meeting gradually evolved into a National Holiness convention that wrestled with such issues as sectional division, theological tensions, new Holiness denominations, and a global mission strategy. Study commissions held seminars for pastors and evangelists

---

29 *Hallelujahs from Portsmouth, or, A Report of Portsmouth Campmeeting held at Portsmouth, R.I. July 23 to August 8, 1897*, Christian Unity Publishing Co., Springfield, MA, 1897, p. 151.

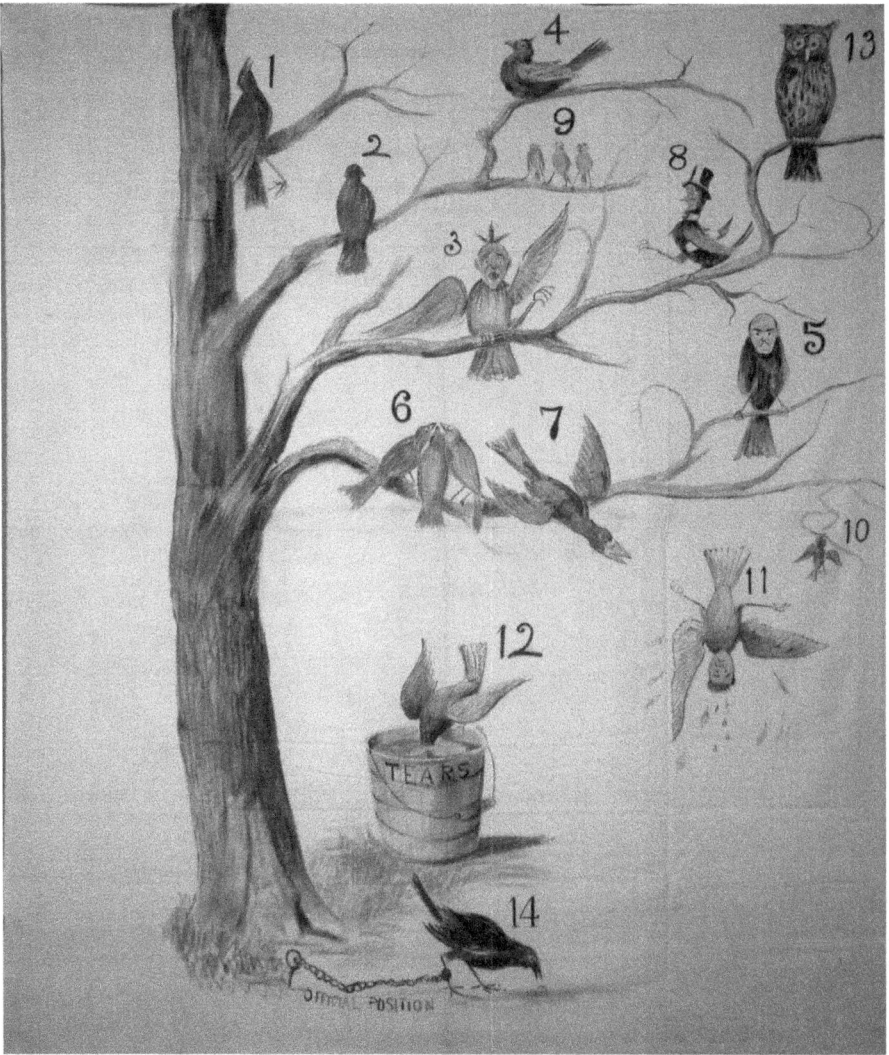

Painted Camp Meeting Illustration for a Unknown Sermon (circa 1900)

Painting from the Arthur Greene collection of the Archives and Special Collections of B.L. Fisher Library, Asbury Theological Seminary

Photo of Pasadena Camp Meeting (1917)

Image from the Archives and Special Collections of B.L. Fisher Library, Asbury Theological Seminary

**Photograph of H.C. Morrison at an Unknown Camp Meeting
(circa. 1910)**
*Image from the Archives and Special Collections of B.L. Fisher Library,
Asbury Theological Seminary*

as well as camp meetings. As a result, the national camp meetings slowly disappeared. Evidence suggests that the last official encampment was held in University Park, Iowa, in 1942.[30]

The gradual decline of Holiness camp meetings in the 1920s and on is probably tied to the growth of Pentecostalism, which emerged on the scene in April of 1906 at the Azusa Street Revival and rapidly spread into various holiness denominations both in the United States and abroad. As Kenneth Brown notes,

> The Pentecostal camp meeting has been an integral part of the revival which produced the modern Pentecostal charismatic movement... Practically every Pentecostal evangelist and denomination used or participated in camp meetings and it became part of the standard fare in Pentecostal revivalism.[31]

African-American Camp Meetings and Influence

The historical information presented in this book so far has focused on the growth and development of camp meetings among the white church primarily. This is not to imply that there were not significant similar movements within the African-American church as well. African-American camp meetings most likely began fairly early in camp meeting history, but little research has been done on the subject and primary sources of these events are rare. Kenneth Brown writes,

> The evidence is strong to support the claim that slaves attended and participated in the Grassy Branch Camp Meeting of 1794, and in successive encampments after that. These black Christians had to conduct their own services, with their own preachers, in their own quarters; in effect, they had to hold their own separate camp meeting. Bishop Francis Asbury encouraged Methodists to minister to the slave population, who in turn eventually founded

30 Kenneth O. Brown, "Christian Holiness Partnership (CHP)," in *The A to Z of the Holiness Movement*, edited by William Kostlevy. Lanham, MD: The Scarecrow Press, Inc., 2010, pp. 52-53.
31 Kenneth O. Brown, *Holy Ground: A Study of the American Camp Meeting*. New York, NY: Garland Publishing, Inc., 1992, pp. 41-42.

their own campground, perhaps as early as the first quarter of the nineteenth century. This encampment also had to relocate several times, but it found a permanent home in 1879, on land deeded to the trustees by Mary E. Tucker. The modern ancestor of the early slave encampment is Tucker's Grove Camp Meeting, named in honor of its benefactor, and located near Machpelah, North Carolina. It has been operated continuously by the African Methodist Episcopal Zion Church since 1876, and is listed on the National Registry of Historic Places. It claims to be the oldest continuously operated black camp meeting in the nation; it can also claim joint honors with nearby Rock Springs as one of the first camp meetings ever held.[32]

It does appear that in the early period of the camp meeting, whites and blacks did sometimes worship together (although perhaps at different times), as found in this early report on a camp meeting by Methodist circuit rider, Jesse Lee in Georgia in 1807 (I have added italics to point out specific points of interest regarding African-American camp meetings).

> The Methodists have lately had a Camp Meeting in Hancock County, about three miles south of Sparta in Georgia. The meeting began on Tuesday, 28th July, at 12 o'clock, and ended on Saturday following. We counted thirty-seven Methodist preachers at the meeting; and with the assistance of a friend I took an account of the Tents, and there were one hundred and seventy-six of them, and many of them were very large. From the number of people who attended preaching at the rising of the sun, I concluded that there were about 3000 persons, *white and black together*, that lodged on the ground at night. I think the largest congregation was about 4000 hearers.
>
> We fixed the plan to preach four times a day-at sunrise, 10 o'clock, 3 o'clock and at night; and in general we had an exhortation after the sermon. We had 14 sermons preached at the Stage; and 9 exhortations given after the sermons

---

32 Kenneth O. Brown, *Holy Ground: A Study of the American Camp Meeting*. New York, NY: Garland Publishing, Inc., 1992, pp. 8-9.

were closed; besides these, there were two sermons preached at the Tents on one night, when it was not convenient to have preaching at the Stage.

The ground was laid out in a tolerable convenient place, containing 4 or 5 acres, and the Tents were pitched close to each other; yet the ground only admitted of about 120 Tents in the lines; the other Tents were pitched behind them in an irregular manner. We had plenty of springs convenient for to supply men and beasts with water. The first day of the meeting, we had a gentle and comfortable moving of the spirit of the Lord among us; and at night it was much more powerful than before, and the meeting was kept up all night without intermission however, *before day the white people retired, and the meeting was continued by the black people.*

On Wednesday at 10 o'clock the meeting was remarkably lively, and many souls were deeply wrought upon; and at the close of the sermon there was a general cry for mercy; and before night there were a good many persons who professed to get converted. That night the meeting continued all night, *both by the white & black people*, and many souls were converted before day.

On Thursday the work revived more & spread farther than what it had done before; and at night there was such a general stir among the mourners at the Stage that we did not attempt to preach there; and as we had but one Stage it was thought best to have preaching at some of the Tents. The meeting at the Stage continued all night and several souls were brought to God before day, and some just as the day broke.

Friday was the greatest day of all. We had the Lord's Supper at night, by candlelight, where several hundred communicants attended; and such a solemn time I have seldom seen on the like occasion; three of the preachers fell helpless within the altar; and one lay a considerable time before he came to himself. From that the work of convictions and conversion' spread, and a large number were converted during the night, and there was no intermission until the break of day. At that time many stout hearted sinners were conquered.

On Saturday morning we had preaching at the rising of the sun; and then with many tears we took leave of each other.

I suppose there was about eighty souls converted at that meeting, *including white and black people*. It is thought by many people that they never saw a better Camp Meeting in Georgia.

The people in general behaved exceedingly well; and there was not a public reproof given from the pulpit during the meeting. There were a few disorderly persons who brought liquors to sell, etc. But the Magistrates took some of them with a State warrant, and bound them over to court; after this we were more quiet. This Camp Meeting will long live in the memories of many of the people who attended it.[33]

Most often, however, the evidence seems to point to the formation of separate camp meetings being formed in the same areas at about the same time.

---

33 *Farmer's Gazette* (Sparta, GA.), Aug. 8, 1807, signed Jesse Lee, reprinted U.B. Phillips, *A Documentary History of American Industrial Society: Plantation and Frontier*. Cleveland, OH: A.H. Clark, 1910, vol. 2: 284–86.

Etching of "A Negro Camp Meeting in the South" from Harper's Weekly (August 10. 1872)

Image in the Public Domain

Illustrations and accounts of the African-American camp meetings mostly come out of the viewpoint of whites and not the African-American community itself. As such, the images are often either romantic on one end or racist and stereotypical on the other end.[34]

One major exception to the segregation of the camp meetings comes especially during the time of the Camp Meeting Association for the Promotion of Holiness (and also during its time as the National Association for the Promotion of Holiness). One of the major speakers and influential women speakers in the white camp meetings of the time was the African-American, Amanda Berry Smith.

Amanda Smith was born into slavery. Her father managed to purchase his own freedom and then worked to pay for the freedom of his wife and children from another slave owner. This would have been difficult, if not impossible, if Amanda Smith's mother had not helped her young mistress, "Miss Celie" with her own experience of sanctification after a camp meeting at Cockey's Campground. Amanda Smith wrote,

> My mother went along to assist and wait on Miss Celie, as she had always done. It was an old-fashioned, red-hot Camp Meeting. These young people went just as a kind of picnic, and to have a good time looking on. They were staunch Presbyterians, and had no affinity with anything of that kind. They went more out of curiosity, to see the Methodists shout and holler, than anything else… The spirit of the Lord got hold of my young mistress, and she was mightily convicted and converted right there before she left the ground; wonderfully converted in the old-fashioned way; the shouting, hallelujah way.[35]

Miss Celie died young, but not before forcing her parents to make a deathbed promise to allow Amanda's father to buy back his family.

---

34 For a recent book from an African-American perspective, see Minuette Floyd's work *A Place to Worship: African American Camp Meeting in the Carolinas* (2018, Columbia, SC: University of South Carolina Press). Floyd's work relates her own childhood at Tucker's Grove Camp Meeting and is supplemented by her photographic work of the modern African American camp meeting.

35 *An Autobiography: The Story of the Lord's Dealings with Mrs. Amanda Smith, the Colored Evangelist*, by Mrs. Amanda Smith, Chicago, IL: Meyer and Brother, 1893, p. 19.

Engraving of Amanda Berry Smith (1893)
Image in the Public Domain

Amanda Smith had a difficult life, losing two husbands and her only two children during her younger years as she supported her family as a washerwoman. She experienced sanctification listening to Rev. John Inskip while sitting at the back of a white church. She would write of her life, "I often say to people I have a right to shout more than some folks; I have been bought twice, and set free twice, and so I feel I have a good right to shout. Hallelujah!"[36]

Amanda Smith noted she attended her first national camp meeting in 1870 in Oakington, Maryland, when she was still working as a washerwoman and had to borrow some money to go, trusting in God's providence to repay it. She wrote in her autobiography,

> That camp meeting I shall never forget. How God gave me friends and blessed me. It was the first time I had ever been to a meeting of that kind. I had never heard such testimonials and such preaching on holiness. The Sunday

---

36 Ibid., p. 22.

morning Love Feast will never be forgotten. The Lord laid it on me to give my experience of how I found the great salvation, and as I spoke He blest me greatly and the people as well. At the close, Brother Inskip said they wanted five hundred dollars- I think that was the amount- for the expenses of the big tent. Some person proposed to divide the amount in shares, so there was a hearty and prompt response, for everybody seemed to be so happy, and in about ten or fifteen minutes they had the amount, and over. I wanted to give something, I was so glad and happy I thought I would like to give ten dollars if I had it, so I said, "Thou knowest, Lord, if I had it I would give it, do put it into somebody's heart to give it for me."

I had hardly uttered the prayer when dear old Brother John McGlynn stood up and said, "Ten dollars for that colored sister that just now spoke."

"Praise the Lord! Thank you, sir," I shouted. O, I felt I could fly.[37]

Of course the issue of racial prejudice was a constant threat. Amanda Smith relates how at one camp meeting a man from Maine was sanctified and released from a life long issue with racial prejudice. She recounts,

It was a wonderful meeting that afternoon. The first thing he saw when he got up and stood on his feet, he said, was the colored woman standing on a bench with both hands up, singing, "All I want is a little more faith in Jesus." And he said every bit of prejudice was gone, and the love of God was in his heart, and he thought I was just beautiful!

I saw him the next year, and he was still saved. And he sat down by me in the dining hall at the table and gave me two dollars; and he said the past year had been the best year of his life. Oh, how happy he was![38]

There was some discussion when there was to be a national camp meeting in Knoxville, Tennessee in 1872. Some wanted Amanda Smith to attend and were willing to offer to pay her way, but others, including the Inskips were opposed, feeling that racial tensions could cause problems in

37 Ibid., p. 67.
38 Ibid., p. 185.

Christian Holiness Association Leaders and Evangelists (late 19th cent.)
Sitting (Left to Right): George Asbury McLaughlin, Amanda Berry Smith, Milton Lorenzo Haney, Unknown, and Charles Joseph Fowler
Standing (Left to Right): Margaret Jenkins Harris, John Millard Harris, and Isaiah Reid
Image Used Courtesy of The Church of the Nazarene Archives

the South. As she was praying about going she asked God for the sign of what she saw as an impossible amount of money- $50.00 as a sign that she was to go. Amanda Smith relates,

> Just as I was to get up from my knees, a suggestion like this came:
>
> "You know the Kuklux are down there, and they might kill you."
>
> Then I knelt down again, and thought it all over; and I said, "Lord, if being a martyr for Thee would glorify Thee, all right; but then, just to go down there and be butchered by wicked men for their own gratification, without any reference to Thy glory, I'm not willing. And now, Lord, help me. If Thou dost want me to do this, even then, give me the grace and enable me to do it."
>
> Then these words came; "My grace is sufficient for thee." And I said, "All right," and got up.
>
> I came up to the tent where I was staying, at Mrs. Little's, with perfect triumph. I never said a word to her, or to anyone.
>
> On Sunday morning at the eight o'clock meeting, which was always a very grand meeting, I arose, and the Lord led me to relate my experience; how the Lord sanctified my soul; and the Holy Spirit seemed to fall on the people in a very powerful manner as I related my experience. And the Spirit said to one lady, "Get Amanda Smith fifty dollars to go to Knoxville."
>
> This lady was the wife of a minister, Rev. Mr. Gardner. She had had a wonderful struggle for the blessing of a clean heart, and she told the Lord when she was consecrating herself to Him, that she would do anything He told her. So when the Spirit suggested this to her, she said, "I'll do it."[39]

With the money in hand, Amanda Smith went and spoke in Knoxville and relates a number of powerful conversions and accounts of sanctification as a result of her speaking and giving her testimony.

---

39 Ibid., p. 207.

Dr. Phineas Bresee, the founder of the Church of the Nazarene, invited Amanda Smith to speak at Asbury Methodist Episcopal Church in Los Angeles around 1891, and he noted,

> She preached one Sabbath afternoon, as I never heard her preach before, and as I have rarely ever heard anybody preach, in strains of holy eloquence and unction, almost equal to Bishop Simpson in the zenith of his power and sacred oratory. The Lord opened heaven on the people in mighty times of glory.[40]

In this quote, he likens the oratory of a former washerwoman, born into slavery with little education or financial backing, to Bishop Matthew Simpson of the Methodist Episcopal Church, considered by some to be the greatest orator of the 19th century, who had the ear of Presidents Lincoln, Grant, and others. Amanda Smith's holiness preaching was surely inspiring in its day at both white and African-American camp meetings.

In her later years, Amanda Smith founded the Amanda Smith Orphanage and Industrial School Home for Abandoned and Destitute Colored Children in North Harvey, outside of Chicago. Smith worked hard at fundraising to make this an institution based on interracial cooperation. Finally due to ill health, Amanda Smith retired to Sebring, Florida, where she died in 1912. The orphanage she founded burned down in 1914 and closed its doors, but the evangelist known as "God's image carved in ebony," had made a lasting impact on the camp meeting movement.

---

40 *Phineas F. Bresee: A Prince in Israel,* by E. A. Girvin, Kansas City, MO: Nazarene Publishing House, 1916, chapter 11.

Chapter 6:

The Decline of the Camp Meeting Tradition

We shall sing on that beautiful shore,
The melodious songs of the blest,
And our spirits shall sorrow no more
Not a sigh for the blessing of rest.
In the sweet by-and-by
We shall meet on that beautiful shore.
In the sweet by-and-by
We shall meet on that beautiful shore.

In the Sweet By-and-By (1868)

- Sanford F. Bennett (1836-1889)

Photo of Frank Stanger at the Redwoods Camp Meeting (circ. 1950)
Image from the Archives and Special Collections of B.L. Fisher Library,
Asbury Theological Seminary

After the National Holiness Association ended doing national camp meetings in 1942, many local and regional holiness associations continued to operate and hold regular camp meetings. The National Holiness Association changed its name in 1971 to the Christian Holiness Association and in 1998 to the Christian Holiness Partnership, but it effectively left the task of camp meetings to the local associations.

Kenneth Brown has argued as late as 1992 that the holiness camp meeting is still active and growing, but he breaks the camp meeting category into three divisions: denominational camp meetings, associational/organizational camp meetings, and interdenominational camp meetings. Brown notes, "It most emphatically is not dying out; new ones are founded almost every year."[41] However, in the past 25 years since Brown's book

41 Kenneth O. Brown, *Holy Ground: A Study of the American Camp Meeting.* New York, NY: Garland Publishing, Inc., 1992, p. 35.

there is little evidence that the camp meeting as a method for evangelism is flourishing. In 2018, the Holiness Camp Meeting Directory online (http://campmeeting.us/) listed only 121 active holiness camp meetings in 23 states. Even assuming camp meetings that may be active and not listed (and not including denominational camp meetings), that probably leaves at most only around 200 active holiness camp meetings in existence today.

With World War II and the growing reality of modern transportation, globalization, communication, and technology, the appeal of the nostalgic camp meeting of previous eras is passing. Despite this reality, the influence of the camp meeting still lingers.

Camp Meeting Music

Perhaps one of the enduring aspects of the camp meeting tradition has been the emotional camp meeting music that continues to impact Christian worship. Early camp meetings used a "call and response" type of singing, which evolved into the traditional style of hymns with verses and choruses. Music leaders would sing a verse and the crowds would respond with the better-known choruses, and often this music would be based on folk or children's tunes which were already known or easily learned. Much of the Church's traditional hymnody in the United States developed from this camp meeting style of singing.[42]

Wheeler notes that in the early camp meetings there was no clear set of music or lyrics, but that did not prevent the crowds from singing! She recounts one writer from 1801, who described it this way,

> A serenade of music cheered all their spirits. Which never desisted from their first coalition until they decamped, and everyone sung what they pleased, and to the tunes with which he was best acquainted; under the sound of this general melody there was a band of preachers... and they with animation, and with powerful vociferation harangued as many as could hear consistent with the melody.[43]

She also points out that the presence of African-American slaves would have introduced white audiences to very different rhythms and especially

---

42 Cf. "The Music of the Early Nineteenth-Century Camp Meeting: Song in Service to Evangelistic Revival," Anne P. Wheeler. *Methodist History* 48(1):23-42 (October 2009).

43 Ibid., 24.

the call-and-response style of singing. Preachers or other leaders would sing verses from simplified hymns and the people would respond with repetitive, easy to learn choruses. Some of these choruses were "wandering" choruses that could be used for different verses and often had little connection to the meaning of the verses.[44] Wheeler notes,

> Instead of relying solely on the strophic hymns and metrical Psalters of their forebears, the people adopted a call-and-response pattern in which verses were supplemented by short refrains and choruses. The standard pattern that evolved took the form of alternating four-phrase verses and repeated choruses, with the preacher or other song-leader singing out the verses and the people joining in the choruses. Verses tended to be simplified versions of traditional hymns, with marked rhythms and often employing a pentatonic scale, or narratives that juxtaposed scriptural texts with personal testimonies. Choruses typically did not rhyme or follow standard metric forms of traditional hymnody, favoring instead the forms familiar in folk and children's tunes. The repetitious nature of the refrains and choruses interspersed with the verses facilitated enthusiastic participation by even the least musical and literate in the group.[45]

In writing about the use of song in the Holiness Camp meetings of the National Holiness Association in 1873, Rev. George Hughes wrote,

> Nowhere is Christian song so rich and so full of moral power, as in the forest temple. The blessed hymns which a succession of holy men have been inspired to write for the comfort and edification of the Church, how they sweep through the groves as with the melody of immortality! It is sublime! The soul is stirred to its profoundest depths. Sinners themselves are spellbound by the magic influence of a sweet song. Many a heart of adamant under its power is melted...

---

44 Ibid., pp. 26-30.
45 Ibid., p. 26.

None, except those who have stood on a National Camp Ground, can have any conception of the effect produced at each opening service, when the president ascends the stand, and commences to sing,

"There is a fountain filled with blood," etc.

Instantly the whole assembly is in unison with the strain, and it is rolled through the forest like a battle-hymn indeed. No tuning-fork or organ is necessary to help the musical flow. The people strike the right key at once, keep excellent time, and onward it moves with wondrous life and energy. The first verse opens to view at once the plentitude of gospel-grace, and the depth and fullness of the fountain of redemption. Each eye discerns it; each heart exults at the unfolding.[46]

There were also common themes in camp meeting music of the time. Wheeler notes especially the use of the words, "Come" and "Farewell." The first songs were designed to encourage the penitent people to come to the altar for forgiveness and restoration, while the "Farewell" songs focused to remind people as they were leaving the camp meeting that they were prepared for a subsequent meeting in heaven due to their association with Christ and his people at the camp meeting. However, the driving concern of camp meeting songs was the salvation of the individual soul.[47]

Wheeler also notes that the camp meeting provided a place for the exchange of musical traditions between both black and white people who attended the early meetings. She writes,

When characteristics of either group served the social and evangelistic purposes of the gathering, they would likely be adopted by members of the other group. Thus the driving rhythms, improvisational style, and call-and-response patterns of traditional African music became a standard practice in the camp meeting assemblies, just as the biblical texts and salvation stories preached in the stand, and the

46 Rev. George Hughes, *Days of Power in the Forest Temple*. Boston, MA: John Bent and Co., 1873, pp. 244-245.

47 "The Music of the Early Nineteenth-Century Camp Meeting: Song in Service to Evangelistic Revival," Anne P. Wheeler. *Methodist History* (October 2009).48(1):31.

stanzas of Watts and Wesley offered up by song leaders, provided new verbal images that made their way into the spirituals of the black community.[48]

In addition, the use of music at camp meetings encouraged the rapid growth and development of songbooks designed especially for camp meetings, which sold in record numbers. If the camp meeting left no other legacy, the fact that most Christians in the United States and around the world sing hymns in a similar style, with verses and choruses, which emerged out of the camp meeting tradition, would argue for the importance of the Methodist and Holiness Camp Meeting Tradition. Of course the legacy is much richer and deeper than the music we use to worship, but the spirit of the camp meeting- the struggle for individual salvation and holiness in all aspects of our lives- remains, even if the camp meeting form itself disappears into history.

Concluding Remarks

On a personal note, I grew up in the environment of the "domesticated" camp meeting. My grandparents owned summer cottages first at Wesleyan Grove in Oak Bluffs, Massachusetts, and then at Hedding Campground in Epping, New Hampshire. My Methodist pastor grandfather preached sermons on these campgrounds, mostly in his younger years, and I have fond memories of vacationing in both places. Yet, it was years before I realized the significance of the camp meeting in American religious history.

I remember my first realization as I took a short cut from my grandparent's cottage at the Hedding Campground to the spring near the center of the grounds. I must have been about thirteen or so as I went with some empty jugs to collect some spring water. As I walked through a wooded area behind some of the smallest and oldest cottages, I realized these cottages did not face the main street, but rather looked back into the wooded area I was walking in. I then realized how many old decaying tree stumps were around me, and how they were cut rather high- just right for laying down boards to make crude benches. Then it dawned on me that this wooded area was shaped like a shallow bowl and only contained young trees as opposed to the large majestic trees in other parts of the campground. In awe I realized that here was where people sat to listen to preachers in days gone by, where they constructed tents and later cottages facing what must have been a crude preaching stand. I felt a kind of holy

---

48 Ibid., p. 34.

Photo of Camp Wofowag and Piano, Connecticut (circ. 1900)
Image from the Archives and Special Collections of B.L. Fisher Library, Asbury Theological Seminary

wonder I had never felt before. God had used this place in ways I could only dream of at that time, but I definitely sensed that I was standing on holy ground!

Is there a future for the camp meeting? I often reflect on that and wonder. As a Christian, I know we do not put our trust, faith, and effort into methods- our focus is on the communication of the Gospel message by whatever method works in any given context. Yet, in our fast-paced world today, people need to learn to disconnect from technology and go out into the creation around us and reconnect with our Creator. We need to recharge our spiritual batteries, not just as individuals, but as a community as well. Since all this is true, perhaps we may yet see another revival of the camp meeting in our own day, or in a future generation. It will probably not look exactly the same- there will be different songs, different activities, different fashions, and different voices, but the Holy Spirit remains the same- and after all, that was the whole point of the camp meeting from the very beginning!

Works Consulted

Allen, Rev. Stephen
 1888 *The Life of Rev. John Allen, Better Known as "Camp Meeting John."* Boston. MA: B.B. Russell.

Asbury, Francis
 1821 *The Journal of the Rev. Francis Asbury, Bishop of the Methodist Episcopal Church, From August 7, 1771, to December 7, 1815.* New York, NY: N. Bangs and T. Mason, Vol. 2.

Blanchard, Charles L.
 1962 *A Study of the Modern Camp Meeting.* M.A. Theology dissertation at the Louisville Presbyterian Theological Seminary.

Brown, Kenneth O.
 2010 "Christian Holiness Partnership (CHP)," in *The A to Z of the Holiness Movement*, edited by William Kostlevy. Lanham, MD: The Scarecrow Press, Inc., pp. 52-53.

 1992 *Holy Ground: A Study of the American Camp Meeting.* New York, NY: Garland Publishing, Inc.

Cole, Scott W.
 2007 *Traumatized Performance: Antebellum Methodist Camp Meetings and the Re-Making of the American Frontier.* Ph.D. dissertation at the University of Washington.

Davies, Edward E.
 1890 *Illustrated History of the Douglas Camp-Meeting.* Boston, MA: McDonald, Gill, and Co.

Floyd, Minuette
2018 *A Place to Worship: African American Camp Meeting in the Carolinas.* Columbia, SC: University of South Carolina Press.

Girvin, E. A.
1916 *Phineas F. Bresee: A Prince in Israel*, by E. A. Girvin, Kansas City, MO: Nazarene Publishing House.

Heitzenrater, Richard P.
1999 "John Wesley's Principles and Practice of Preaching," *Methodist History* (January) 37(2): 89-106.

Hough, Henry Beetle
1936 *Martha's Vineyard: Summer Resort 1835-1935.* Rutland, VT, The Tuttle Publishing Company, Inc.

Hughes, Rev. George
1873 *Days of Power in the Forest Temple.* Boston, MA: John Bent and Co.

Lander, John K.
2003 *Itinerant Temples: Tent Methodism 1814-1832.* Studies in Evangelical History and Thought. Waynesboro, GA: Paternoster Press.

Lee, Jesse
1807 *Farmer's Gazette* (Sparta, GA.), Aug. 8, 1807, signed Jesse Lee, reprinted in U.B. Phillips, *A Documentary History of American Industrial Society: Plantation and Frontier.* Cleveland, OH: A.H. Clark, 1910, vol. 2: 284–86.

Mead, Amos P., ed.
1859 *Manna in the Wilderness: Or, The Grove and its Altar, Offerings, and Thrilling Incidents: Containing a history of the Rise of Camp-Meetings, and a Defense of this Remarkable Means of Grace, also an Account of the Wyoming Camp Meeting.* Philadelphia, PA: Perkinpine and Higgins.

Pike, J.M., ed.
    1894   *The Double Cure, or Echoes from National Camp-Meetings.* Boston, MA: McDonald and Gill Co.

Red River Meeting House web site: http://www.rrmh.org/history.

Rees, Seth, W. D. Woodward, and Byron J. Rees, eds.
    1897   *Hallelujahs from Portsmouth, or, A Report of Portsmouth Campmeeting held at Portsmouth, R.I. July 23 to August 8, 1897,* Christian Unity Publishing Co., Springfield, MA.

Richey, Russell E.
    2015   *Methodism in the American Forest.* New York, NY: Oxford University Press.

Rogers, James R.
    1910   *The Cane Ridge Meeting-house.* Cincinnati, OH: The Standard Publishing Company.

Rogers, John
    1847   *The Biography of Eld. Barton Warren Stone, Written by Himself; with Additions and Reflections.* Cincinnati, OH: J.A. and U.P. James.

Salter, Darius
    2003   *America's Bishop: The Life of Francis Asbury.* Nappanee, IN: Evangel Publishing House.

Smith, Amanda
    1893   *An Autobiography: The Story of the Lord's Dealings with Mrs. Amanda Smith, the Colored Evangelist.* Chicago, IL: Meyer and Brother.

Strickland, W.P.
    1853   *Pioneer Life in the West: The Autobiography of James Bradley Finley.* Cincinnati, OH: Cranston and Curts. Digital version accessed at: http://wesley.nnu.edu/wesleyctr/books/0601-0700/HDM0683.pdf.

Trollope, Frances Milton
    1832   *Domestic Manners of the Americans.* London: Printed for Whittaker, Treacher, and Co.

Various Authors
    1993   *Special issue of Christian History,* issue no. 38, "George Whitefield: 17th Century Preacher and Revivalist."

Vincent, Rev. H.
    1870   *History of the Camp-Meeting and Grounds at Wesleyan Grove, Martha's Vineyard, For Eleven Years Ending with the Meeting of 1869.* Boston, MA: Lee and Shepard.

Wheeler, Anne P.
    2009   "The Music of the Early Nineteenth-Century Camp Meeting: Song in Service to Evangelistic Revival," *Methodist History* (October) 48(1):23-42.